CHICAGO PUBLIC LIBRARY
CONRAD SULZER REGIONAL LIBRARY
4455 LINCOLN AVE.
CHICAGO, ILLINOIS 60625

JUV/
F
868
.S156
B75
2001

SULZER

Chicago Public Library

W9-DEY-469

Angel Island

DEC   2001

Cornerstones of Freedom

Angel Island

LARRY DANE BRIMNER

CHILDREN'S PRESS®
A Division of Grolier Publishing
New York • London • Hong Kong • Sydney
Danbury, Connecticut

Reading Consultant: Linda Cornwell, Coordinator of School Quality and Professional Improvement, Indiana State Teachers Association

Content Consultant: Katherine Toy, Executive Director, Angel Island Immigration Station Foundation

Visit Children's Press on the Internet at:
http://publishing.grolier.com

Library of Congress Cataloging-in-Publication Data

Brimner, Larry Dane
  Angel Island / Larry Dane Brimner.
    p. cm.—(Cornerstones of freedom)
  Includes index.
  Summary: Describes the history of San Francisco Bay's Angel Island as an army base, detention center, and immigration station before its preservation as a state park.
  ISBN 0-516-21566-3 (lib.bdg.) 0-516-27278-0 (pbk.)
  1. Angel island—History—Juvenile literature. 2. San Francisco Bay Area (Calif.).—History Juvenile literature. [1. Angel Island (Calif.)—History. 2. California—History.] I. Title. II. Series.
F868.S156B75 2000
979.4'62—dc21
                                                99-14957
                                                   CIP

GROLIER
PUBLISHING

©2001 Children's Press®
A Division of Grolier Publishing Co., Inc.
All rights reserved. Published simultaneously in Canada.
Printed in the United States of America.
1 2 3 4 5 6 7 8 9 10 R 10 09 08 07 06 05 04 03 02 01

從今遠別此樓中
各位鄉君眾歡同
莫道其間皆西式
設成玉砌變如籠

Detained in this wooden house
for several tens of days,
It is all because of the
Mexican exclusion law
which implicates me.
It's a pity heroes have no way of
exercising their prowess.
I can only await the word so that
I can snap Zu's whip.

RU7070701/
CHICAGO PUBLIC LIBRARY
CONRAD SULZER REGIONAL LIBRARY
4455 LINCOLN AVE.
CHICAGO, ILLINOIS 60625

From 1910 to 1940, Angel Island Immigration Station was the main point of entry into the United States for tens of thousands of Asian immigrants. Located in California's San Francisco Bay, Angel Island was designed to receive both Asian and European immigrants. In 1917, the United States entered World War I (1914–1918). As a result, the expected flood of European immigrants in California did not take place, but Asian immigrants continued to arrive. About one-third of the immigrants processed on Angel Island came from China to seek their fortune in California. They called California Gum Saam—the land of the Golden Mountains. One-third came from Japan, and one-third came from other places, including Russia, Europe, and Central and South America.

The Angel Island Immigration Station in the early 1900s

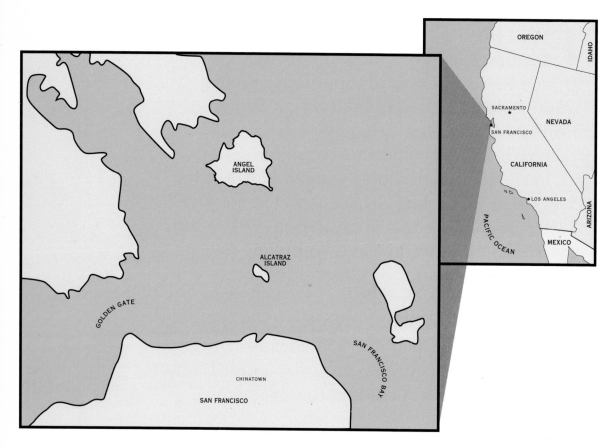

This map of the San Francisco Bay area illustrates Angel Island's isolated location.

Unlike New York's Ellis Island, an immigration center that welcomed European immigrants to American shores, Angel Island did not welcome the Chinese. Although it was called the "Ellis Island of the West," the Angel Island Immigration Station excluded, or kept out, as many Chinese people as possible. While other immigrants arriving at Angel Island were examined and allowed to enter the United States with only a brief delay, the Chinese were often held and questioned for long periods of time. From the wooden dock on the island's remote northern shore, thousands of them were deported, or sent back to their homeland.

To better understand why so many Chinese were deported from Angel Island, it helps to know something about the long and painful history of Chinese immigration to the United States. It began around 1848, when gold was discovered in California. At that time, wars and poverty in China forced many Chinese to leave their homeland. There were wild stories about San Francisco—for example, that the streets were paved in gold—and many immigrants came to California. Like other immigrants, the Chinese—mostly young men in their teens and early twenties—hoped to strike it rich. Most of them never planned to spend their lives in California. They hoped to return to China someday as wealthy and respected men.

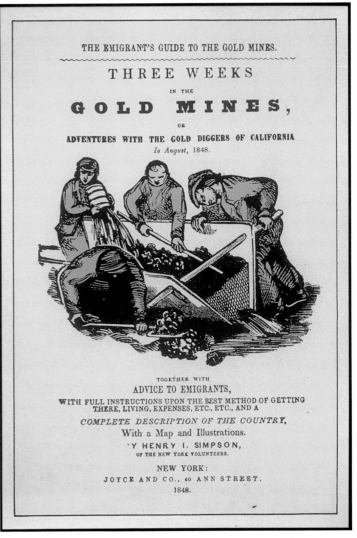

The publisher of The Emigrant's Guide to the Gold Mines *encouraged Asians to buy this instructional book by suggesting that they would strike it rich in California.*

Gold mining was hard work. Chinese gold miners usually worked together and shared their low earnings.

Very few got rich, however. When the Chinese arrived in California's goldfields, they were allowed to work only in sites that white miners had abandoned. Chinese miners were also forced to pay a foreign miner's tax. This tax made up more than half of the tax money collected in California between 1850 and 1870.

Other laws were also passed to make life miserable for the Chinese. Low earnings and high rents meant that many Chinese immigrants had to live together, often crowded into one small room. In 1870, the city of San Francisco passed a law requiring that rooms rented to Chinese people have a certain amount of space per person. Fewer people could live together and housing became more expensive. California did not turn out to be a golden land for most Chinese.

The Chinese did jobs that other people would not do. When the U.S. government decided to

build rail lines across the nation, more workers were needed. The men who founded the Central Pacific Railroad—Leland Stanford, Collis Huntington, Charles Crocker, and Mark Hopkins, also known as the "Big Four"—put out a call for laborers. The Chinese answered this call. They proved to be hard workers, and many were skilled with explosives. This was a useful skill because the tracks would be laid through the rugged Sierra Nevada mountains, and workers had to blast rock to make way for the tracks.

Even so, the Chinese were not treated like the other workers. When Congress passed the Pacific Railroad Act in 1862, it promised the Big Four land and money based on how much track was laid. To speed up the project, explosives were sometimes set off on purpose before the Chinese workers could get clear of the blast. Many Chinese lost their lives laying the tracks through towering mountains and across treeless deserts, but that did not stop the Big Four. They simply hired more workers from China. Some 9,000 of the 10,000 workers on the Central Pacific project were Chinese immigrants.

The Big Four, from left to right: Leland Stanford, Collis Huntington, Charles Crocker, Mark Hopkins.

These Chinese immigrants worked on the Northern Pacific Railroad in the 1880s.

Many people in the United States were not friendly to the Chinese. European immigrants were given a warmer welcome because their customs were similar to the Americans'. After the Central Pacific and Union Pacific railroads connected in Promontory, Utah, on May 10, 1869, people's dislike of the Chinese turned to out-and-out racial hatred. Although the country now had a transcontinental railroad, the California economy slumped. When many Californians did not have jobs, they blamed the problem on the increasing number of Chinese because they were willing to work for lower pay. Tempers flared, and Californians demanded that Congress pass laws restricting Chinese immigration. The popular slogan of

This 1870 cartoon shows that Californians thought the Chinese were taking away their jobs. The illustration suggests that Chinese immigrants were stealing work from this Californian shoemaker and food from his family.

the day was "The Chinese must go!"
In response, Congress passed the Chinese Exclusion Act of 1882. For the first time in American history, an entire ethnic group was refused entry into the United States. The Exclusion Act attempted to stop Chinese immigration—except for a small group of "exempts," or people who were permitted to enter the United States. The exempts included officials, shopkeepers, teachers, students, and tourists. Some Chinese wives and American-born Chinese children were also exempt.

The exemptions gave the Chinese a way to enter the country. Many came as members of the exempt classes. Others claimed a right to enter the United States because their parents were lawful American residents or citizens. Many of these claims were not truthful. When an earthquake struck San Francisco in 1906, the Hall of Records was destroyed. With it went all the records of marriages, births, and deaths. This made it easy for Chinese residents to claim citizenship and to tell immigration authorities that they had more children than they actually had. Then the residents were given the papers needed to bring family members from China. These papers listed a specific number of family members permitted to enter the United States—based on what the so-called citizen had told authorities. There were almost always extra family members listed so they could sell the extra "slots." Chinese immigrants who bought these slots became known as "paper sons" or "paper daughters" because their relationship to the residents existed only on paper.

The cost of a slot was about $100 per year of age. Many young Chinese men wanted the opportunities that the United States promised. They often paid as much as $2,000—an enormous amount of money in those days—to come to California. One paper son spoke about the cost of his own slot in *Island: Poetry and*

History of Chinese Immigrants on Angel Island, 1910–1940: "All the papers then were false and cost $100 per year of age. I was actually 17, but the paper said 19." His payment of $1,900 bought him the papers he needed to immigrate to the United States, but it did not guarantee that he would be permitted to enter. First, he would be detained, or held, by immigration officials. The newcomers stayed in a wooden, two-story shed on a dock owned by the Pacific Mail Steamship Company.

After a long journey across the Pacific Ocean, Chinese immigrants arrive in California.

Soon after their arrival, the immigrants were given medical examinations. Most of the people came from areas in China where health conditions were poor, so many immigrants had illnesses. The officials said that people with certain illnesses were not healthy enough to stay in the United States. Only immigrants who passed their medical examination were allowed to proceed to the next step—the interrogation process. Then officials examined their papers and interviewed witnesses who might—or might not—support their claim. The questioning process could last from two weeks to two months. In some instances, immigrants were held for years before a decision was reached.

The Pacific Mail Steamship Company shed was far from an ideal place to hold immigrants.

Immigrants had to stand and wait their turn to be examined by a doctor.

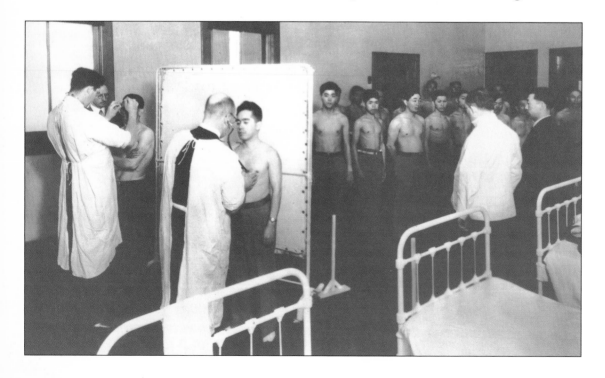

Its location near San Francisco's Chinatown meant that answers to the officials' questions could easily be smuggled to immigrants who were trying to enter the United States under false claims. With as many as five hundred people crammed into the dark, upstairs quarters at one time, the shed was filthy and unsafe. Also, escape was easy for anyone determined to get out of the shed. *The San Francisco Examiner*

A street in Chinatown in 1925

reported on September 9, 1908: "Using common . . . knives and a rough saw made out of a knife, eleven Chinese cut their way out of the detention shed . . . early Monday morning and made their escape." On March 24, 1909, the *Examiner* again reported a breakout, this one cut short by three security guards who discovered that "iron bars nearly an inch thick were sawed through, and the strong wire netting with strands nearly half an inch in thickness were [cut] . . . and [sixty-two] eager Chinese were [about to gain] their liberty." Those who did escape usually disappeared into Chinatown.

For years, Chinatown's leaders had complained bitterly about the shed's conditions. Even San Francisco's leading newspapers called it "squalid," or filthy. In 1903, the Bureau of Immigration finally agreed and announced that it would build a new immigration station— on the north shore of Angel Island. The bureau's decision had little to do with any concern for Chinese immigrants, though. While planning ahead for the expected wave of European immigrants, the bureau wanted to stop the frequent escapes by Chinese immigrants and the smuggling of information from Chinatown to them. San Francisco Bay's rough waters and Angel Island's distance from Chinatown promised to solve all the bureau's problems.

The Angel Island Immigration Station is located on the northeast corner of the island.

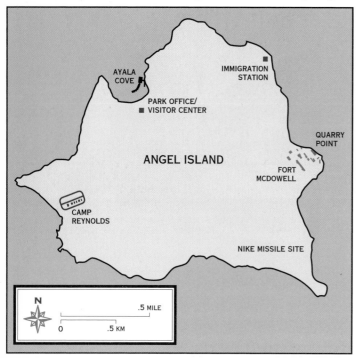

Chinatown's leaders objected to the location. They complained that the new immigration station was too far from San Francisco. Within months of opening the immigration station in 1910, the government came to its own

14

conclusions about Angel Island. Its isolation made it expensive to run. Everything—from food to workers—had to be brought in by boat. In addition, there was a limited amount of drinking water, and there were not enough bathrooms for the detainees, or people held in custody. On top of those problems, the station's wooden buildings were fire hazards. Even so, the government refused to move the station back to San Francisco. For the next thirty years, newly arrived immigrants were held at the Angel Island Immigration Station.

Immigrants were held in this building on Angel Island. Now it is a museum and a national historic landmark.

Some Asian men worked in California orchards. This man is tending an irrigation ditch.

Chinese immigrants were not the only Asians to be held in the Angel Island Immigration Station and the Pacific Mail Steamship Company shed. These were also points of entry for a flood of Japanese immigrants. In the beginning, they were mostly young men, and many of them were farmers or fishermen. At first, they were accepted, even if they were not wholeheartedly welcomed to California. When California's economy slumped in the late 1800s, they, like the Chinese, were blamed for the hardships. California farmers, fearing the competition, called for a ban on all Japanese immigration, which led to the Alien Land Law of 1913. It barred land sales to aliens who were not permitted to be citizens—and foreign-born Asians could not become citizens. Neither the Alien Land Law nor the persistent pressure on lawmakers stopped Japanese immigration.

At that time, arranged marriages were traditional in Asia. Family members in Japan often chose wives for the young Japanese men living in California. The new brides set sail for the United States, where thousands of them met their husbands for the first time on the dock at Angel Island. These Japanese women were called "picture brides" because the men identified their brides by pictures sent ahead. The steady flow of picture brides and Chinese exempts made it look as though the Exclusion Act was not working. Californians demanded that the so-called "yellow peril" stop.

This 1920 photograph shows Japanese picture brides waiting to meet their new husbands at Angel Island.

Imagine how afraid these Chinese women and children must have been. They were separated from their family, kept in a fenced area, and guarded by an American woman.

New arrivals to Angel Island were told to leave their luggage and all their belongings in a warehouse on the dock. They marched up the hill to the wooden, two-story dormitory, or building, where they would live while they were there. They were given medical examinations soon after landing. Those who passed the medical exam and whose papers appeared to be in order, such as Japanese picture brides, were allowed to collect their belongings and go ashore within a few days. Most Chinese immigrants, however, were not given permission to enter. Instead, they were held on Angel Island. Immigration authorities were on the lookout for "paper sons" and "paper daughters" and wanted to stop anyone from entering the country with false papers. As a result, they tried to prove whether each detainee's story was true through a series of interviews.

While they waited for their interviews, the detainees lived together in a drafty dormitory, surrounded by barbed-wire fence to prevent escapes. Lights were turned out at about

9:00 P.M., and the doors were locked from the outside by a guard.

The detention was a long and lonely time for the immigrants. Men and women, including husbands and wives, were separated. They were not allowed to talk to each other until the interviews were completed and entry was granted. The detainees passed their time playing games or reading Chinese-language newspapers brought in from Chinatown. At that time, Chinese men were more likely than women to have some education. Many men wrote poems on the walls of the dormitory that told about their journey to the United States. Many of the poems criticized the way the Chinese were treated. Most Chinese arrivals, however, spent their detainment looking out across the bay and wondering why they were locked up "like criminals."

This Chinese poem is carved in the walls of the dormitory at Angel Island. The poem's author complains about being held in the wooden building. The author writes that he is innocent and has been treated unfairly.

Privacy did not exist in the dormitory. Between two hundred and five hundred Chinese were held at Angel Island at any given time, and each was assigned a bed in a long row of steel bunks stacked three high. A small courtyard outside the dormitory gave the immigrants an opportunity to stretch and walk, but it was fenced in with barbed wire. At mealtimes, guards marched the immigrants into the dining hall, locked the doors, and kept watch as the detainees ate their tasteless meals.

The poor quality of the food angered many detainees. The kitchen staff and supplies were provided by a company that got the job because it charged the lowest prices. As a result, the quality of the food was poor. In an effort to

The bunks in the crowded dormitory were narrow, and the mattresses were thin.

change this and other conditions, a few detainees formed a group called the Chinese Self-Governing Organization. Although the organization had no real authority, its members met with immigration officials to ask for changes. When nothing was done, the group organized food protests. Usually, these protests were nothing more than refusals to eat or cafeteria food fights, and the press rarely reported them. The most noticeable result was a sign written in Chinese warning detainees not to make trouble or spill food on the floor. In 1919, however, one protest became a full-fledged riot. Soldiers from Fort McDowell, on another part of the island, were called in to stop the riot. After that, the quality of the food improved.

These two men worked in the kitchen at Angel Island in the early 1900s. Kitchen staff members often told immigrants news from Chinatown.

The kitchen staff, mostly from Chinatown, could do little about the quality of the food they were hired to prepare, but their presence on Angel Island was a link between the detainees and Chinatown. Kitchen helpers brought news from Chinatown, including Chinese-language newspapers. More important, they smuggled in answers to interview questions, something Angel Island's isolation was supposed to prevent.

In their effort to catch any detainee attempting to enter with false papers, immigration officials usually had three interviews with a new arrival. Each interview was long—sometimes lasting three hours or more, and the same questions were asked again and again. How many streets does your village have? How many houses are in your village? Where is the rice bin kept in your house? Is there a clock? How many windows are in your house? Which direction does the door face? Is there a family pet? How many chickens did you own? How many stairs lead up to the family house? What is your family history? These questions were meant to be tricky and were cross-checked by interviewing the detainee's so-called family members from Chinatown. One wrong answer could be cause for deportation.

To prepare themselves for the interviews, Chinese immigrants studied "coaching books" on their voyage from China. These were purchased along with their false papers and, like answers to a test, they gave detailed information about the so-called father's village, family, and house. Usually, the coaching books were tossed overboard before the ship arrived in San Francisco Bay, but now and then some were smuggled into the Chinese dormitory. One detainee reported that he'd studied his coaching notes for a whole summer before he left China.

Then he sewed them inside his cap, hoping he could refresh his memory from time to time before his interview. He said, "I never had a chance to look at them, because you're among people all the time and you don't trust anyone. There was no private place where I could be alone to study them. One time, they [the other detainees] were playing catch with my cap and they didn't understand why I was so upset. I was scared." If his coaching notes had been discovered, he would have been sent straight back to China.

Immigration officials question an immigrant while a Japanese picture bride waits her turn.

This page from a coaching book tells immigrants how to answer questions about their village in China.

Sometimes, if more interviews were scheduled, detainees arranged for the information they needed in another way. Leaders of the Chinese Self-Governing Organization would get questions to the kitchen help who would then smuggle the answers back to the dining hall—for a fee. Sometimes the answers were hidden under a soup bowl, inside a newspaper, under the peel of an orange, or even in a peanut shell!

Discovery of coaching notes could end a detainee's dream of life in the United States, so smuggled notes were highly guarded. Most information got to the detainees, but now and then a note was discovered. This March 20, 1928, article from the *San Francisco Chronicle* points out how important coaching notes were at the Angel Island Immigration Station: "An attack by fifty infuriated Chinese upon Mrs. Mary E. Green . . . when she discovered and seized a . . . note which they were attempting to pass to a Chinese girl in the dining room was revealed yesterday . . . " Detainees recovered the note from Mrs. Green, and immigration authorities never saw what it said. In spite of Angel Island's isolation, the smuggling of information was no more difficult there than in the Pacific Mail Steamship Company shed.

Angel Island had other flaws too. Immigration officials and Chinese interpreters working for the government were not always trustworthy. An article in the October 6, 1915, *San Francisco Chronicle* said that two interpreters bribed a man named George Wong, saying he would have to pay them $200 or they would translate his wife's words incorrectly so that she would be deported. The January 22, 1917, *San Francisco Examiner* reported that "[h]igher-ups appear to have [directed] the loss of . . . individual records of Chinese from Angel Island through a period of many years." Two days earlier, an article in the *San Francisco Chronicle* had discussed the importance of these stolen records: "This theft of the records would [make it possible for] a clever attorney to bring into this country Chinese who had no right of entry, but whose descriptions fit . . . the descriptions on the stolen records."

The fire that destroyed the administration building on August 12, 1940, led to the closing of the Angel Island Immigration Station.

Plagued by scandals and complaints, Angel Island Immigration Station's end was unavoidable. When a fire broke out on August 12, 1940, the administration building was destroyed. The island's last immigrants—about two hundred people—were transferred to a new location in San Francisco, and Angel Island Immigration Station was closed. The decision to close it was not the result of a sudden change of heart about the Chinese, however. It was mainly the result of politics. It would have been too costly to rebuild the administration building. Also, the U.S. government wanted a better relationship with China in the 1940s, so the Chinese Exclusion Act was politically embarrassing. The act was finally repealed in 1943, when China and the United States were at war with Japan.

After the closing of the immigration station, Angel Island served many other purposes. It held prisoners of war during World War II (1941–1945). In 1954, the state of California purchased the island and founded Angel Island State Park. One year later, a missile base was established on the southeast tip of the island.

These missiles were installed on Angel Island in 1955, but they were removed for safety purposes when Angel Island State Park was enlarged.

Today, people enjoy having picnics at Angel Island State Park.

The Angel Island Immigration Station was almost forgotten. Eventually, more people learned that it excluded Chinese immigrants rather than welcomed them. In 1970, a park ranger, Alexander Weiss, rediscovered the poems that covered the dormitory walls. The poems touched the hearts of Asian-Americans and, thanks to their efforts, the building escaped scheduled demolition, became a museum, and was named a national historic landmark in 1997. Many of today's visitors to Angel Island State Park are children and grandchildren of the Chinese immigrants who lived in the dormitory.

Experts are not sure how many immigrants came to Angel Island, but there may have been from 175,000 to 400,000. Roughly one-third of these were Chinese who, like the flood of European immigrants entering through Ellis Island, hoped to find a better life in the United States. Instead, many Americans tried to deny Chinese immigrants that opportunity, and they suffered greatly. Today, the poem-covered walls at what was once the Angel Island Immigration Station stand as silent but eloquent testimony to their despair.

GLOSSARY

alien – a foreigner

citizen – a member of a political body, such as a country, who has the right to live there

deport – to expel or banish from a country

detain – to hold or to keep in custody

Angel Island dormitory

detainee – a person held in custody

detention – being held in custody

dormitory – a building where a group of people live

economy – a country's industry and trade

entry – a way into a place

exclude – to keep out, shut out, or leave out

exempt – free or excused from a duty or rule that applies to others

immigrant – a person who leaves a homeland to settle in a foreign country

immigrate – to come to live in a foreign country

Officials interrogate an immigrant.

interpreter – a person who translates foreign languages

interrogate – to question closely

interview – a meeting in which one person asks another questions

isolation – being set apart or separated from others

slot – a place or position

TIMELINE

1848 Gold discovered at Sutter's Mill, California, and Chinese immigration begins

1862

Pacific Railroad Act paves way for transcontinental railroad, and thousands of Chinese workers are hired

1882 Chinese Exclusion Act restricts immigration

1910 Angel Island Immigration Station opens

1913 Alien Land Law bars land sales to aliens

1914
1918 } World War I prevents European immigration to California, but Asian immigrants come

1940

1941
Prisoners of war held on Angel Island during World War II
1945

Angel Island Immigration Station closes after fire destroys administration building

Angel Island State Park founded **1954**

Missile base established **1955**

Alexander Weiss rediscovers poems that covered dormitory walls **1970**

1997 Angel Island Immigration Station becomes national historic site

INDEX (*Boldface* page numbers indicate illustrations.)

FOR FURTHER INFORMATION

Angel Island Association
P.O. Box 866
Tiburon, CA 94920
http://www.angelisland.org

Angel Island Immigration Station Foundation
P.O. Box 472243
San Francisco, CA 94147
http://www.aiisf.org

PHOTO CREDITS

Photographs ©: Archive Photos: 7 left, 7 far left (American Stock), 7 right (Kean), 7 far right; California Department of Parks and Recreation: 23, 30 bottom (Angel Island State Park), cover, 11, 27; California Historical Society: 18; California State Library, History Section: 16; Chris Huie: 3, 19, 21, 24, 31 bottom; Corbis-Bettmann: 2, 15 (Philip Gould), 17, 26, 31 center left (UPI), 6, 8, 31 top; Liaison Agency, Inc.: 13 (Hulton Getty); National Archives at College Park: 12; Robert Fried Photography: 1, 20, 28, 30 top; Stock Montage, Inc.: 5, 9.

Maps by TJS Design.

PHOTO IDENTIFICATIONS

Cover: Immigrants arrive at Angel Island in the early 1900s.
Page 1: A view of Angel Island from the water
Page 2: Poems and other writings were carved into the wooden walls of the immigrant detention center on Angel Island. The center is now a museum, and the poems have been translated for visitors.

ABOUT THE AUTHOR

Larry Dane Brimner is a former California teacher and teacher-trainer who has taught at all levels, from elementary to graduate school. He now writes full time for children and is an award-winning author of more than seventy-five books, including several titles for Children's Press. Mr. Brimner lives in San Diego, California, and Rico, Colorado.